# SCHIRMER'S LIBRARY
## OF MUSICAL CLASSICS

Vol. 1794

# ANTONIO VIVALDI

## Six Sonatas

### For Violoncello and Piano

Realized and Edited by
NIKOLAI GRAUDAN

**G. SCHIRMER, Inc.**

DISTRIBUTED BY

**HAL•LEONARD®**
CORPORATION
7777 W. BLUEMOUND RD. P.O. BOX 13819 MILWAUKEE, WI 53213

# PREFACE

The original manuscript of the six sonatas *á Violoncello solo* by Antonio Vivaldi (in the Bibliothèque Nationale of Paris) consists of 42 pages on which the cello part and the bass (not figured) are written very neatly and plainly on two staves. There are but a few instances in the musical notation which might be considered slips of the pen. In contrast, many of the bowings are inaccurate and approximate.

In order to present a true picture of Vivaldi's manuscript the cello part of the piano score has been left un-edited, except for the inevitable adjustment of the position of the slurs. The bass is original, but it has sometimes been moved an octave lower or doubled. The few corrections in the text are clearly indicated.

The editor's additions to the original text are an attempt to clarify the musical content of the sonatas and to facilitate its realization. Three types of additions will be found:

1. *tempo* definitions have been made more specific, and some descriptive terms have been added,

2. *dynamic* markings have been provided,

3. additional *bowings* have been indicated.

In this task, the guiding considerations were as follows:

a. Vivaldi limited himself in this work to the use of *Largo* and *Allegro* only. In other compositions he made the tempo indications more precise by adding terms like *poco, molto, non tanto, con moto* and many others. He sometimes also indicated the character of a piece by such expressions as *dolce, amoroso, spiritoso* and others.*

b. there are no dynamic marks whatsoever in the manuscript. In other works Vivaldi used a great variety of shadings in the full dynamic range from *pp* to *ff*.*

c. the bowings in the manuscript seem to have been jotted down hastily, more as a hint for the articulation desired than a practical direction. Often, it is not even possible to be certain exactly to which notes the slurs belong, nor are they always used consistently. Nevertheless, they are of great importance and value to the performer in offering a clue to the composer's intentions. A good example of the originality of his ideas is the articulation in the second Largo of the *third sonata,* one of the instances where it is shown clearly. The bowings as printed in the cello solo part, while following the indications of the manuscript as closely as possible, are designed to preserve the articulation and to provide at the same time a practical solution for it. They should also aid in attaining expressive and sensitive phrasing. They presume, of course, a judicious use of the bow as to exact part and length to be applied in each instance.

Explanation of some bowing marks:

a. notes with dots under a slur ⌢ are short, those with dashes ⌢ are long with but a slight separation,

---

* See Walter Kolneder, Aufführungspraxis bei Vivaldi. Breitkopf & Härtel, Leipzig 1956/7.

b.  **......** denotes a clear separation between the notes with the bow resuming **its** movement in the same direction,

c. where two different bowings are marked in the last bar of a movement, the upper is to be used before the repeat, the lower for the ending.

Ornaments:

a. the sign ⌁ stands for a trill, long or short, usually to begin with the auxiliary note,

b. the suggested execution of grace notes is indicated above the text.

These sonatas deserve a high place in the cellists' concert repertoire, but they are also singularly well suited for teaching purposes because of the many technical and musical problems they offer. One should strive especially to search out the individual character of each movement and thus recreate the sonatas in their full life instead of presenting a merely "correct" rendition. Only in this way can one do justice to the great inventive and emotional power with which Vivaldi has endowed these compositions.

Nikolai Graudan

# Sonata No. 1

Realized and edited
by Nikolai Graudan

Antonio Vivaldi
(1678 - 1741)

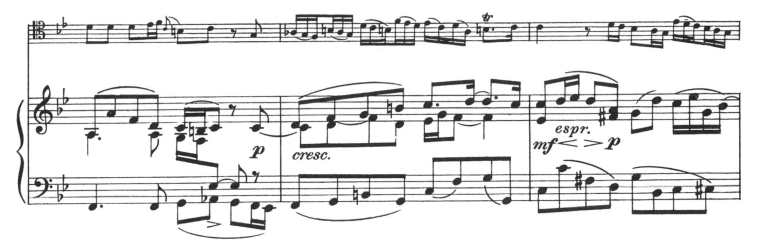

**Allegro**

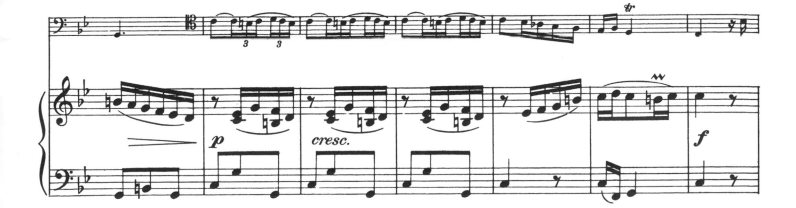

Largo (maestoso)

Allegro (gaio)

# Sonata No. 2

44409

Allegro (deciso)

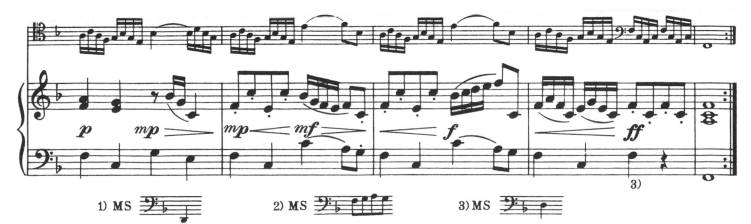

1) MS 𝄢  2) MS 𝄢  3) MS 𝄢

44409

Largo (non troppo, amoroso)

**Allegro (con brio)**

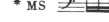

* MS

44409

# Sonata No. 3

Largo

Violoncello

# SCHIRMER'S LIBRARY
## OF MUSICAL CLASSICS

Vol. 1794

# ANTONIO VIVALDI

## Six Sonatas

### For Violoncello and Piano

Realized and Edited by

NIKOLAI GRAUDAN

## G. SCHIRMER, Inc.

DISTRIBUTED BY

HAL•LEONARD®
CORPORATION

7777 W. BLUEMOUND RD. P.O. BOX 13819 MILWAUKEE, WI 53213

# Sonata No. 1

**Violoncello**

Realized and edited
by Nikolai Graudan

Antonio Vivaldi
(1678-1741)

44409 cx

# Violoncello

Largo (maestoso)

Violoncello

Allegro (gaio)

# Sonata No. 2

Largo (non troppo, amoroso)

Allegro (con brio)

Violoncello

# Sonata No. 3

44409

# Violoncello

# Sonata No. 4

# Violoncello

# Sonata No. 5

Allegro (con spirito)

# Sonata No. 6

Largo (doloroso)

non troppo forte ma molto sentito

**Allegro (energico)**

Largo

Allegro (Allegretto moderato, poco giocondo)

44409

# Sonata No. 4

Largo (Andante sostenuto)

44409

Allegro (vivace)

44409

Largo (mesto)

44409

Allegro (quasi Allegretto)

# Sonata No. 5

Allegro (ma non troppo)

Largo (doloroso)

Allegro (con spirito)

# Sonata No. 6

Largo

Allegro (non troppo)

Largo (doloroso)

*MS

Allegro (spiritoso)